T0400785

THE CLIMATE CRISIS IN
THE SOUTHWEST

by Brienna Rossiter

FOCUS
READERS.

NAVIGATOR

WWW.FOCUSREADERS.COM

Focus Readers is distributed by North Star Editions:
sales@northstareditions.com | 888-417-0195

Produced for Focus Readers by Red Line Editorial.

Content Consultant: Douglas Kenney, PhD, Director of the Western Water Policy Program at the University of Colorado Boulder Law School

Photographs ©: Shutterstock Images, cover, 1, 8–9, 11, 18; Rick Bowmer/AP Images, 4–5; Phil Millette/US Fish and Wildlife Service/NIFC, 6; Red Line Editorial, 13; Natural Hazards/USGS, 14–15; Southwest Biological Science Center/USGS, 17; Felicia Fonseca/AP Images, 21; iStockphoto, 22–23, 25; Lauren B. Smith/Danita Delimont/Alamy, 27; Ross D. Franklin/AP Images, 29

Library of Congress Cataloging-in-Publication Data
Library of Congress Cataloging-in-Publication Data is available on the Library of Congress website.

ISBN
978-1-63739-636-0 (hardcover)
978-1-63739-693-3 (paperback)
978-1-63739-801-2 (ebook pdf)
978-1-63739-750-3 (hosted ebook)

Printed in the United States of America
Mankato, MN
082023

ABOUT THE AUTHOR

Brienna Rossiter is a writer and editor who lives in Minnesota.

TABLE OF CONTENTS

CHAPTER 1

Dangerously Dry 5

CHAPTER 2

Typical Climate 9

CHAPTER 3

Many Impacts 15

THAT'S AMAZING!

Navajo Water Project 20

CHAPTER 4

Solutions 23

Focus on the Southwest • 30
Glossary • 31
To Learn More • 32
Index • 32

DANGEROUSLY DRY

In January 2020, states in the Southwest faced extreme dryness. Water levels in rivers and lakes dropped. Temperatures soared. The hot, dry weather fueled wildfires. In Colorado, huge fires burned. Many homes and forests were destroyed. Smoke from the fires spread hundreds of miles. It made the air unsafe to breathe.

By 2022, water levels in Utah's Great Salt Lake had reached all-time lows. Some docks were left without water.

In 2020, the Cameron Peak Fire and East Troublesome Fire became the two largest wildfires in Colorado history.

The dry period lasted through August 2021. It was the region's worst drought since 1895. Scientists linked the extreme conditions to **climate change**.

In addition, Lake Mead and Lake Powell were drying up. These are the two largest **reservoirs** in the United States. In 2021, they reached record lows. Some people had their water supplies cut off.

In 2022, most of the Southwest became extremely dry again. Rivers and lakes dropped even further. The region faced even worse water shortages.

News outlets called both dry periods *droughts*. This term wasn't wrong. The periods were drier than normal. However, the Southwest has been getting drier since 2000. So, the droughts were part of a longer trend. Scientists did not expect that trend to stop. Instead, the Southwest was becoming permanently drier. This process is called **aridification**. Climate change was the main cause.

CHAPTER 2

TYPICAL CLIMATE

The Southwest's climate is warm and dry. However, the amount of **precipitation** varies. This difference is partly from El Niño and La Niña. These weather patterns are based on the temperature of the Pacific Ocean. El Niño happens when the ocean is warmer. It brings more moisture to the Southwest.

Climate describes long-term weather patterns. For example, a desert may have rainy weather one day. But its climate is still dry.

When the ocean is cooler, La Niña makes the Southwest drier.

Conditions also depend on location. The region has deserts, plains, plateaus, and mountains. As the elevation changes, the climate does, too. Elevation is the height of land compared with sea level. The southern part of the region has hot, dry deserts and plains. The plateaus tend to be cooler and rainier. They are higher up and farther north. The Rocky Mountains are even higher and cooler.

The Southwest is the driest and hottest US region. As a result, water is often in short supply. Much of the region's water comes from snowpack. This snow builds

Utah's Canyonlands National Park is in the Colorado Plateau.

up in the mountains during winter. Then it melts in the spring. It flows down from the mountains. It fills lakes, streams, and rivers.

The Southwest's climate has also varied with time. Scientists have tracked average temperatures and rainfall over the past 100 years. Some wet or dry periods last for decades. From 1905 to 1930, the region was much wetter than usual. But it was very dry from 1942 to 1956. This variation has been happening for many years. The Southwest had a series of huge droughts between the years 1000 and 1450.

CLIMATE TRACKING

Some scientists use computers to track and study climate conditions over time. This practice helps them learn what changes are and aren't normal. Scientists use particular methods for studying recent years. For example, they might use data collected by weather stations. However, methods are different for studying the more distant past. Then scientists might look at tree rings. Trees grow new rings each year. During wet years, rings are wide. Rings from dry years are narrow.

However, recent years are outside the usual range. The Southwest has had more heat and less rain than ever before. Climate experts say these changes are caused by human actions. **Greenhouse gas emissions** are the main cause.

THE SOUTHWEST

CHAPTER 3

MANY IMPACTS

Climate change is affecting the Southwest. Aridification is one major threat. Many plants and animals are already at the high end of how much drought they can withstand. Even small changes can make it hard for them to survive. In the 2000s, for example, many piñon pine trees in New Mexico died.

These photos show the drying out of a New Mexico piñon forest between 2002 (left) and 2004 (right).

Average temperatures in the Southwest are already rising. And scientists predict even warmer and drier conditions in the future. These changes increase chances of heat waves and droughts. They can also make these events last longer. Extreme heat can make people sick. It raises demand for water, too. As a result, shortages become more likely.

Higher temperatures also reduce the snowpack. That can lower water levels in rivers, lakes, and streams. These bodies of water depend on the melting snow. Some years might have less snow. Or the snow might melt earlier. Then water in reservoirs can run low or dry up.

The lighter areas of the rock show how much water levels in Lake Powell had dropped by April 2022.

When that happens, crops and animals can run out of water.

As temperatures rise, the ranges of plants and animals can shift. Some move to higher elevations. They may harm or crowd out other plants and animals. For example, bark beetles are killing trees throughout the Southwest.

As more grasses spread to the Sonoran Desert and more wildfires burn in the region, saguaro cacti could die out.

Wildfires spread more easily in hot and dry weather. They can become bigger and more frequent. Large fires damage land and buildings. They also pollute the air with smoke.

Even the life cycles of plants and animals can change. Warmer weather can make flowers bloom earlier. Animals may change the times when they move to new homes. In some cases, the new timing can kill them. It also harms people who rely on them for food. For example, some **Indigenous** peoples harvest corn, acorns, and salmon. If these foods disappear, people's health and traditions are impacted.

BIGGEST IMPACTS

Indigenous people tend to be most impacted by climate change. Tribal lands are often located in dry areas. In many cases, the US government forced people to move and stay there. Residents may have a hard time getting access to water. Droughts make this problem worse.

NAVAJO WATER PROJECT

Emma Robbins is a Diné artist and activist. Diné people are also known as the Navajo. Robbins helps run the Navajo Water Project. This organization helps people get access to water. It often focuses on the Navajo Nation reservation. Robbins grew up there. At least 30 percent of homes on it have no running water. People use pumps or wells instead. But these often run dry. Many are **contaminated** by uranium. This metal came from old US government mines.

Robbins wanted to bring clean, safe water to her community. However, the problems were complex. People on the reservation often face poverty and lack of funding. **Racism** plays a

A member of the Navajo Nation uses a pump to fill up a water drum in his truck.

role, too. The US government often ignores tribal rights.

The Navajo Water Project has ways to overcome these challenges. The group uses a community-led approach. By 2022, it had set up nearly 300 home water systems on the reservation. It also had set up more than 1,400 storage tanks.

CHAPTER 4

SOLUTIONS

Many ways to fight climate change exist. Renewable energy is a major one. Renewable sources include wind and sunlight. They produce power without releasing greenhouse gas emissions.

The Southwest has many sunny days. For this reason, solar power is a good option. By the early 2020s, Utah and

Solar panels produce electricity in the Sonoran Desert in Arizona.

Arizona were leading states in solar power.

Distributed solar energy systems are also useful. These systems do not use large power plants. Instead, they produce power near where it will be used. Colorado has programs for this type of power. The programs help people put solar panels on the roofs of their homes. People can sell any extra electricity to power companies.

These efforts can slow climate change. But they won't stop it completely. People must adapt to changing conditions.

Conserving water is important. Individuals can work to use less water

A worker installs a solar panel on a roof in Denver, Colorado.

in their homes and yards. But bigger changes are also needed.

For example, agriculture uses most of the Southwest's water. Many ranchers in the area raise cattle. Cows eat crops such as hay and alfalfa. These crops use large amounts of water.

Scientists point to a few possible solutions. One is raising fewer cattle.

Then farmers can grow fewer crops. Instead, they can practice fallowing. They would skip planting crops for at least one season. The land then needs less water. Government programs can support this practice. States can pay farmers to fallow. That way, farmers won't lose money.

In addition to water, addressing wildfires is important. One method is controlled burns. These fires help lower the risk of large wildfires. This practice was once common. Indigenous peoples used controlled burns for thousands of years. But the US government stopped these burns in the 1900s. That change helped increase wildfires. Controlled

A farm growing wheat in Colorado is fallowing part of its fields.

burns started coming back in the late 1900s. Many tribes helped lead this effort.

Other changes focus on protecting vulnerable groups. Children, the elderly, and low-income people tend to be most at risk. These groups face greater health risks from heat waves and pollution. But they often have fewer ways to deal with them. They may also have trouble getting enough food or water. Cities across the Southwest are working to help. Many cities have set up food banks and community gardens. They help people get the resources they need to stay safe and healthy.

PHOENIX FIGHTS THE HEAT

Phoenix, Arizona, is the hottest major US city. In 2010, the city started a new project. It aimed to plant thousands of trees across Phoenix. But by 2021, little progress had been made. Meanwhile, heat-related deaths in Phoenix kept rising. That year, the city created a new department to focus on heat. One team helped unhoused people reach cooling centers. Another mission focused on trees and shade.

Unhoused people stay in a cooling center in Phoenix, Arizona, during a 2022 heat wave.

Where people live can put them at risk, too. Buildings in large cities trap heat. They create extra-hot areas known as urban heat islands. To protect people who live in these places, cities can plant trees. The trees' shade keeps areas cooler.

The Southwest is facing a serious climate crisis. But more and more people are working to help.

FOCUS ON
THE SOUTHWEST

Write your answers on a separate piece of paper.

1. Write a paragraph summarizing some of the harmful effects that climate change is creating in the Southwest.

2. Water can be scarce in the Southwest. In the area where you live, what resource is most important to protect or conserve? Why?

3. Which part of the Southwest has the lowest elevation?
   A. the deserts in the south
   B. the Rocky Mountains
   C. the plateaus in the north

4. Which period in the Southwest's history was the hottest and driest?
   A. 1000 to 1450
   B. 1905 to 1930
   C. 2000 to 2020

Answer key on page 32.

GLOSSARY

aridification
The slow change of a region from a wetter climate to a drier climate.

climate change
A human-caused global crisis involving long-term changes in Earth's temperature and weather patterns.

contaminated
Made dirty or unsafe by having something else mixed in.

greenhouse gas emissions
Gases that are released into the atmosphere by factories, cars, and other sources, leading to climate change.

Indigenous
Native to a region, or belonging to ancestors who lived in a region before colonists arrived.

precipitation
Water that falls from clouds to the ground. It can be in the form of rain, hail, or snow.

racism
Hatred or mistreatment of people because of their skin color or ethnicity.

reservoirs
Human-made lakes used for water supply storage.

TO LEARN MORE

BOOKS

Harrison, Audrey. *Arizona*. Minneapolis: Abdo Publishing, 2023.

Huddleston, Emma. *Adapting to Climate Change*. Minneapolis: Abdo Publishing, 2021.

Thacher, Meg. *Using Solar Farms to Fight Climate Change*. Lake Elmo, MN: Focus Readers, 2023.

NOTE TO EDUCATORS

Visit **www.focusreaders.com** to find lesson plans, activities, links, and other resources related to this title.

INDEX

agriculture, 25–26
aridification, 7, 15
Arizona, 13, 24, 28

Colorado, 5, 13, 24
controlled burns, 26–27

drought, 6–7, 12, 15–16, 19

heat waves, 16, 27

Lake Mead, 6, 13
Lake Powell, 6, 13

Navajo Nation, 20–21
New Mexico, 13, 15

Phoenix, Arizona, 13, 28

Robbins, Emma, 20
Rocky Mountains, 10, 13

snowpack, 10–11, 16

Utah, 13, 23

wildfires, 5, 18, 26

Answer Key: 1. Answers will vary; **2.** Answers will vary; **3.** A; **4.** C